Let Us Sit Upon the Ground

poems by

Daniel Rattelle

Finishing Line Press
Georgetown, Kentucky

Let Us Sit Upon the Ground

Copyright © 2017 by Daniel Rattelle
ISBN 978-1-63534-257-4 First Edition
All rights reserved under International and Pan-American Copyright Conventions.
No part of this book may be reproduced in any manner whatsoever without written permission from the publisher, except in the case of brief quotations embodied in critical articles and reviews.

ACKNOWLEDGMENTS

Columbia Review: "Green River Elegy"
pamplemousse: "Landscape With Jugs; Greensboro Bend, VT"
Sigma Tau Delta *Rectangle*: "On the Shoulders of Minor Poets"
Dappled Things "Cantiamo"

Special Thanks to Jack Christian, Michael Filas, Leah Nielsen, Libby and Martha Wassmann and Woody Woodger.

Publisher: Leah Maines

Editor: Christen Kincaid

Cover Art: Martha Grace Wassmann

Author Photo: Libby Wassmann

Cover Design: Elizabeth Maines McCleavy

Printed in the USA on acid-free paper.
Order online: www.finishinglinepress.com
also available on amazon.com

Author inquiries and mail orders:
Finishing Line Press
P. O. Box 1626
Georgetown, Kentucky 40324
U. S. A.

Table of Contents

On The Shoulders of Minor Poets 1

Three Georgics 2

Laundromat; 3 pm March Fifth. A Friday 7

Landscape with Jugs; Greensboro Bend, VT 9

Cantiamo 11

All My Friends Are Dead 12

Saga 13

Propempticon for Woody 15

Facts Not Things 17

Here I dreamt I was a Pre-Raphaelite 19

Another Station, A Different Metro 20

A Young Man Considers the Tyranny of Time and Change;
    Woodstock N.H 2008 21

Green River Elegy 23

Prospects for Resurrection 25

Stations 26

A Minor Ecstasy 27

and the sea across daubed rock evacuates its dead
—Geoffrey Hill

On The Shoulders of Minor Poets
"Isn't it a lovely day, Mr. Bukowski?"

So there we stood, stoned in the garden, and still as statuettes. The primroses glistened with dew. Looked like rain. Hank, drunker than I was, pulled a luger from his belt. I pointed a rifle straight at his head. "Hank," I said, "isn't time we made our peace? I ain't scared to blow your head off." Hank stumbled. Smiled. Fired twice. Brain and heart. I dropped dead. And there I lay in the new mud of early spring, hidden by Hank's gnarly hedges. Later, half sober, he called up a buddy. They rolled me up in some tarp and duct tape. Tossed me in the trunk, then off the nearest bridge. I floated down the river a while, not sure how long, let's say six days, until I washed up on a farm where Wendell Berry's dog unrolled my tarp. I was bloated and green. She sniffed my leg and I knew I was done for. Instead, she leaned me up against a tree and ran to get her master.

Three Georgics
"it's not elves, exactly"

1. Sapling

We felled the alder, work was done.
Then back through knee-high grass
to the spot where we'd begun
that morning, up before the sun,

November air like nicks of glass
on my tendril sapling lungs.
I swear sawdust was stuck
up in my nose and ears for weeks.

Heaving cords into my uncle's truck
seemed a bit too much work
for just a little heat.
Mild season, any luck.

I still can't get that smell out of my nose;
coffee gone stale on flannel
coats, chain-oil and burnt-match tobacco.
I gagged at my smoke soaked clothes

but noon-bread went down like manna
from God in a bluster of snow.
The saws sang out their shape-note hymns
as I saddled a stump and munched

the bread. My cocoa steamed the brim
of a mug. Some snow stuck on to a sawn-off limb,
but with one kick the dust
wisped off like petals from a stem.

In spring I sliced the frosted ground—
with my father's spade—in rows.
I sewed some seeds from an old bag I found.
I screwed the rows and scattered them around

and wondered how anything grows
as tall as that tree we cut down.

2. Sugaring

It was close to dark with one last run to do.
I rode in back with the plastic barrel;
The sap inside sloshed with every bump.
I was youngest by half so it fell to me to trudge

to the furthest tree along the trail,
to unhook and dump the brimming pails.
The woods were hazed in mist that only March
could make; it tangled up in birch

and maple boughs, still bare like old bones
that made me shake. I spat, turned up
my collar and slung my haul, ten gallons
on a yoke across my shoulders.

And back in the shack the boiler ripped;
the air hung thick with sugar-soot.
There was some chatter and glasses clinked,
but I just drank and watched the shadows stretch.

Though dim I could make out a photograph
nailed to a beam, half obscured
by a pair of skis, crossed above the door,
their golden paint faded to stately beige.

My uncle, still green leaned
against his father, flannel coats,
knitted caps and snow-packed mustaches.
His cart was pulled by oxen, they said,

'till '88, or was it '89?
(I was a bit drunk, I admit—
a half-pint of snow-banked whisky.)
So *Yankee Magazine* came up one year

before the first ox took sick and died.
They followed the cart on snow shoe
to snap some shots of aging men
tip pail on pail of sap into a barrel.

I sat on the ground and stared, The others
lit the lamps. My uncle sat in a padded
metal chair and said little
but stoked the fire and sipped a beer.

He rolled a cigarette and smoke
mixed with smoke as sunlight finally failed
and all was left were some headlights,
shadows, and the odd, off-color joke.

3. Stopping My Car by Mayval Farm One Night Recently

I guess I didn't know that cows could sleep.
I guess I thought they stood all day and night
so dumb the only thing they did was munch
on grass then puked it up and chewed the cud,

until they fattened up enough to get
shot-gunned in the back, then chopped up and bagged.
But not tonight. They slept in one big pile
of spotted flesh, the waves of heat like fumes

of dung rose up into the starry sky.
I stopped the car to watch them sleep and tramped
across the road to where they lay and ran
my hand across their bone-chill fence. I gazed

up at the stars and rasped.
Because to tell the truth I couldn't judge
between Orion's belt, either dipper
Polaris and the Pleiades and yeah

it's nice that I had stopped there, sure, but it was cold
and I had work to do. I scraped
back to my car, turned on the heat and checked
my phone. I breathed another sigh
and texted back that I'd be home in five.

Laundromat; 3 pm March Fifth. A Friday
"come then domestic muse"

The tiles are chipped like teeth
and the clock won't tell the time
but keeps the tick. I buy
detergent from a vending machine.

The neighbors upstairs yell in French.
It stinks like fish.
The others speak English
in public. Mihn's knitting and Jimmy

tries the pac man. Mrs. Martinez
starches some Dickies.
The old fluorescents jaundice
the place and remind me

I have to pick up a some bourbon
and a pack diapers while I'm out.
I keep tapping on the vinyl
chair from the 80s

with the beat of the clock, counting
the accents of every thought. I think
it's getting on the others' nerves.
Sitting in the laundromat.

I crank that beast up to high speed
cause I got stuff to do later—
Grey steel and cinderblock no time
for avocado enamel or wallpaper.

I think the heat turns my best shirt pink
and that's embarrassing,
so I watch water wash and enjamb lines
and dryers full with blankets

and the towels
with the high thread count.
So soft.
So absorbent.

Landscape with Jugs; Greensboro Bend, VT

We breathed in dew
from the rye patch in clouds,
vapor like baking
soda on our tongues.

With heavy soles, lonesome
on the path through the potters field—
this northern Hesperides.
The alpacas looked on

with contempt
as we scrambled their orchard
not stopping for an apple
or to tie a shoe.

Over the dingle,
the wind sticky with barley,
we swilled beer jugs
on the lawn

and leaned against the barn
like leaky casks, spiles moldy,
the yeast like chalk on fingers and thumbs.
We'd bagged the valley

below like a sack
of asparagus, wilting,
when the rain began to fall,
just enough to muddy the parking lot

and moisten our brows:
asperges me, domine
hyssopo et mundabor
The fog rolled in between

green hills (an earthen censor.)
I knelt in the mud; a modern
Antaeus, negative-rendered
on a terra cotta pot.

Cantiamo

Well, yeah I'd lie under the Umbrian sun with you
in spring. We'd clutch the grass in easy fists
while the yearlings graze by the vineyard.
Many times would I follow you thigh deep
into the Adriatic. Foreign Land.
Forget that we've never breathed the same air!
or, shirtless, howled duets on Pisan nights.
Caged Bird. Firing Squad. Hang it all,

Ezra Pound,
here is a sign again. I found you,
head like an axe, hidden under ancient vines
your shirt unbuttoned stained with mud
and wine. I said, "I'm afraid you're becoming quaint"
and you, "You whoreson dog! Let's to music!"

Making a bundle of broken vines
I laid them under your head
and gathered grape leaves in a basket
and scattered them over your corpse
and pressed one in your hand
and smeared mud on your ears
and eyes and
lips.

All My Friends Are Dead
i.m. Geoffrey Hill

Like the last Lancastrian king I sat
in the stacks on the fourth floor
re-shelving and nearly done.

The elevator churned like a gut
fed on rats and bread and
I think it's Fallstaff's ghost
drunk on sack. Or is it Richard
come to kiss my ring?

Your book was the grimace
on the shelf. Your eyes like cows'
Your hair shorn like death row.
You died this spring
or so I read on the jacket.
And I found "Requiem," written for me.

Because I have tramped naked
among the sheep.
I too, long to be the subject
of a King or documentary.
I too have clutched my beads
without making a scene.

Will you have gone to the dark unmourned?
If not to Beatrice, to Virgil's bosom
This side of stygian shores.
I'll make you a coracle, at least. Adorned,
with raven quill ribs and strong vellum skin
the perfect casket to set you in,
like a Mercian King, covered in swords.
Only this is left: lend me yours?

Saga

Sing, graybeards, my dreams of ice,
the mead still wet on my lips
the kiss on my cheek

when we sat on our bags in the gate
en route to Reykjavik.
Your sweater was grey,

knit loose like chain mail.
I thought you where an elf-queen.
And at Thingvellir,

breath like iron and running,
having misread the meter,
I stood like Scarp-Hedon, fit

for battle, your dress fallen
like so many leaves in October
which rot-steady in the mulch-heap

behind the shed. Your ash
tree skin was sticky with pitch
like the hull of a viking ship

and I'm at the helm. Sailing Midgard
to Valhalla, because when I rolled
over I couldn't help but think

of Gunnar and Hallgerd
and Njal's black bones reeked
smoke the morning after.

And of the figures that lingered
where we laid down and crushed
back the heather.

So by now I think I know
what Morrissey meant
about girls and graves

but I'm willing
to take a chance.
By the way

could you just shut
the damper on the stove
before coming to bed?

Propempticon for Woody
> *quae tibi creditum*
> *debes Vergilium.* –Horace; Odes I.3

Don't fret the freight
trucks come speeding past, blasted
on reds. Don't fret silence in the cab
on the three hour stretch between

Ithaca and Troy when the music stops
but the whole thing seems too important
to switch disks and anyway the rain
bows your roof Paganini on a riff. Don't fret

the road. Do you remember, there's a mountain
in the Berkshires with a campfire
where Melville took Hawthorne.
I think there's a cave

there too. I really would like to have gone
skating with them on the pond,
not so thick that water couldn't push
back against your steps. And there's a diner

with too-hot coffee whenever you want it.
Back when Jove was a Pizza guy
And old twenty-bags out of the back—
was it vanity that made a prudent god

mingle grass and pavement? Leave it
to me to put my feelings on the page.
You know I'd rather hang around like fog
on the ankles of an April morning,

unbothered by all this bone,
exempt from the duty to make
anything wet but the grass.
All this to say, colleague, forget

Prometheus, but remember
the crows that'll peck your eyes
and scrape your guts
all over the sunlit cliff

like a rabbit broken open
on the highway.

Facts Not Things

Try to imagine him now—Ludwig—
with broad brimmed hat and apron
grubbing among the potatoes

before matins, and he seems happy
though the abbot won't let him
flagellate. He has been given

a seven knot cincture, though,
secured like a tourniquet
around his waist.

Now think of him at the front,
mud erupting, two stepping
on the edge of Ockham's razor,

planting bullets into fertile brains,
toes curled over the lip
of the abyss. These are facts.

I've heard it said that our muses are kin.
Maybe, but then I keep thinking
St. Augustine, quaking for his laurels,

or Plato who lit up his manuscript
at his master's feet. By now I've dropped
a few rungs in Socrates' book.

Meanwhile, back at Oxford, the dust
is getting thick on the teapot,
and there is only one bite

taken from the macaroons
on Russell's desk, arranged
so beautifully by Mrs. Apollinax.

And once, by chance in London
Wittgenstein split a cab
with Wyndham Lewis.

And they went their separate ways
at Kensington Gardens without words
beyond, "good day sir," and "likewise."

But whom will I chase after
down the lane, crying out
"wait, sir, you've forgotten your gloves?"

Here I dreamt I was a Pre-Raphaelite

I got drunk last Wednesday
and, you know they say
some poets see visions of William Blake.
Not me.
I saw a guy who I thought
was Dante Gabriel Rossetti.

I sallied out into the night;
spotted him through a lighted window,
and we sized each other up
through the white-cross pane
like the sons of some other brotherhood.

His pants were stained with mud
and his spade leaned against the porch
from where he had dug up *The House
of Life* from its grave. And damn it
if I had Christina's number in case
things got out of hand.

With one hand he caressed
his hepatic gut. Yellow bloat.
The other upturned a bottle;
wicker basket rotgut.
and I was taken in by this like opium
smoke that no one will say they notice.

So I took up my pentangle shield,
my sword still warm with dragon's blood
and trod across the battlefield
to the willow lined riverbank, to wield
songs instead of swords on my lute, blameless
and trusty, to woo and kneel
and be tempted by red haired maidens in distress
to various and sundry degrees of success.

Another Station, A Different Metro

This station: a mess of flesh and 40oz
bottles drunk to the label.

The guy nodded off, that's okay though.
He'll wake with sound of the train

come screaming from who-can-read
that-map-anyway. The vagrant doesn't

interest me as much as investment bankers
with newspapers they chuck in those bins

as soon as they're done with the finance section.
And the thing that struck me about Eliot's

letters about wading through the glut
of poetry are his praises

of forgotten poets.
This isn't the track to immortality.

A Young Man Considers the Tyranny of Time and Change; Woodstock N.H 2008

> *The red, pre-cambrian light is gone*
> *like imperial Rome, or myself at seventeen- Auden*

So there we stood like crumbs
dropped on a forest walk.
In shallow stream our bones

chilled hopping from rock to rock.
We had some lights to bring us home
just in case we got stuck

or carried away like small stones
tossed and smoothed in the stream.
Lonesome is better than being alone.

An early sickle-moon gleamed,
the loons honked and flew south
above a firing line of trees,

hemlocks, mostly. We hopped our route
back to camp as evening failed,
but we paused at a cut out

cliff of glacier scratched shale.
You read the lines like sheet music,
each epoch a change of scale.

I stood, stoned and clueless.
White water consumed my ankles
and the roar was muted

but nothing like tranquil.
I climbed a tree lain across the water
and scraped up palms in the scramble.

The wind gave me a shudder.
The river choked with leaves.
And to think some trees do this every autumn.

So I clung fast to the bark, the stream's
hiss like a voice long forgotten
then heard again, somewhere unexpectedly.

Green River Elegy
1985-2015

I saw you among poppies, full lotus.
I was throwing cans into the river—

I don't think you noticed.
Here comes Charon now, honking at his harp.

Got dem blues done rattle mah bones
dipping his stick into the dark.

Good thing I stuck a drachma in
your mouth. Fare paid you stepped

aboard the gloomy boat. *Dem bones.*
For once I was at a loss for words

When they told me how they found you
did you haunt the lonesome tracks?

Your shorn head pressed flat against
The window, like a monk at prayer.

Lonesome then, did you come to a mean end?
Did the cops take you for so many bums

sleeping off a drunk? Did they, by instinct,
jam their Narcan up your nose

and give it one last-ditch spray?
But what do I know? Even still

I'll call you Bodhisattva Bill.
I jackknifed a can and jammed

it full of incense; made that piece
belch smoke for days.

But couldn't I have poured you
just one more cup of tea? I got

the kind you like; two baggies,
but you, me, and Dem Bones make three.

I'm reaching buddy, I know it
but I can still see the gondola's wake

and can't help wading knee deep
into the muck to scream the words

of *Amazing Grace* into the passing water

Prospects For Resurrection
And my poor fool is hanged! No, no, no, life! - Lear

When I came home beat and low, and stripped
off my coat and black tie like a corn husk,
and chucked them in the closet with the broom,

I set the kettle to rest, fast against
the iron grate and slow flame like one day
you sat on your heals and poured dragonwell.

You in my tattered *Cordelia's Dad* shirt
and underwear, hair tucked behind your ears.
Or at night, wrapped in linen and snug in

the lilacs, clipped grass clung to your feet, cool
like persimmons or gin soaked gums. Breakfast
was tea and toast. When you spooned the honey

you uncovered a bee's wing, preserved,
incorrupt like a saint before the last horn blows.

Stations
>*For Martha*

I had my eye on the second station
when I got the call and I wondered
if, when they laid the cross upon His back,
the splintered wood which made His muscles burn,

your namesake hunkered down in the kitchen
and busied herself with piles of flatbread,
if she punched and stretched out her grief
like a lot of dough and just a little yeast.

It was winter though. I'd just come inside
from splitting wood in my *Smiths* shirt, the snow
packed and mixed with mud beneath my boots,

each slice of birch or elm rang out like bells
at Mass, when I heard you had sewn
some birdseed for your very lucky birds.

A Minor Ecstasy

So
A river ran through a patch of red pines,
A small river-a stream some might say
Its water was clear, white, we saw bottom
When we peered from the mossy embankment.
We walked there one day, waylaid,
Taking leave of other travels.
The fine needles of the forest floor
Shone with the first frost of the season.
And as the midday sun pierced the trees,
A mantle of mist lay over our bare feet.
In silence, except the sound of the stream,
We stood and watched the water pass:
Toda ciencia trascendiendo.

Notes

The title of this chapbook is from *Richard II* Act 3 Scene 2.

The epigraph for the chapbook is from "Requiem for the Plantagenet Kings" by Geoffrey Hill.

The epigraph on "On the Shoulders of Minor Poets" is from "The Last Days of the Suicide Kid" by Charles Bukowski.

The epigraph on "Three Georgics" is from "Mending Wall" by Robert Frost

Ezra Pound's retort in "Cantiamo," is from his "Sestina: Altaforte"

The epigraph on "Laundromat; 3 pm March Fifth. A Friday" is from "Washing Day" by Anna Laetitia Barbauld.

The epigraph on "A Young Man Considers the Tyranny of Time and Change" is from "A Walk After Dark" by W.H Auden.

The epigraph on "Prospects for Resurrection" is from *King Lear* Act 5 Scene 3.

The final line in "A Minor Ecstasy" is the refrain in "The Ecstasy of Contemplation" by Saint John of the Cross.

"Facts Not Things" is for Bob Gruber, who chose the better part.

It may be of interest that: Mayvall Farm is in Westhampton MA; Cordelia's Dad was a folk punk band from Amherst MA; The Green River runs through Greenfield, MA.

Daniel Rattelle grew up in Western Massachusetts where he still lives with his wife and two kids. He studied writing at Westfield State University. His poetry has recently been published in *Measure, the Saint Austin Review, Columbia Review, pamplemousse, Dappled Things* and elsewhere. This is his first chapbook.

www.ingramcontent.com/pod-product-compliance
Lightning Source LLC
LaVergne TN
LVHW051614080426
835510LV00020B/3283